The Visual Guide t

Asperger's Syndrome and Communication

by Alis Rowe

Also by Alis Rowe

One Lonely Mind
978-0-9562693-0-0

The Girl with the Curly Hair - Asperger's and Me
978-0-9562693-2-4

The 1st Comic Book
978-0-9562693-1-7

The 2nd Comic Book
978-0-9562693-4-8

The 3rd Comic Book
978-0-9562693-3-1

The 4th Comic Book
978-15086839-7-1

The 5th Comic Book
978-15309879-3-1

Websites:
www.thegirlwiththecurlyhair.co.uk
www.thecurlyhairconsultancy.com
www.theliftingplace.com

Social Media:
www.facebook.com/thegirlwiththecurlyhair
www.twitter.com/curlyhairedalis

The Visual Guide to

Asperger's Syndrome and Communication

by Alis Rowe

Lonely Mind Books
London

For people on the autism spectrum and the people around them

hello

Good communication isn't just about exchanging information, it's about being in tune with somebody else and considering how they might be feeling and what they might be wanting to say.

Believe it or not, many people (with or without an Autism Spectrum Disorder) aren't very good at communicating! We can all learn some helpful tactics from this guide!

This guide will cover some of the essentials of good communication, as well as look at some relevant things to be aware of when the exchange is between an autistic person and a neurotypical person.

What stands out most to me is that there is responsibility on both people to make a communication meaningful and productive. Therefore, in this guide, although I've touched on what neurotypical people can do to help people with ASD, I've also suggested some things people with ASD can do to help.

I hope you learned as much from this guide as I learned from writing it!

Alis aka The Girl with the Curly Hair

Contents

WHAT IS COMMUNICATION?

Communication is the exchange of information

It is thought to occur via three channels: words, tone of voice, body language

The general belief is that most communication occurs through body language, followed by tone of voice, and only a small amount through the use of words

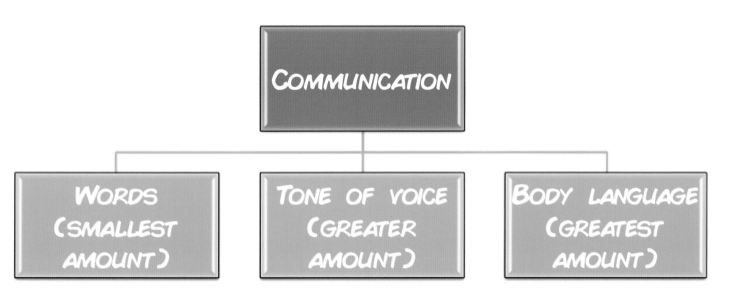

These proportions often surprise people!

Body language, tone of voice, and the ability to understand someone else's body language and tone of voice are likely to be impaired in an autistic person

When communicating with a person with ASD, it might be helpful therefore, to pay extra attention to words as these are of extra importance

A SIMPLE EXAMPLE MIGHT BE THE GIRL WITH THE CURLY HAIR NOT RECOGNISING THAT HER MUM IS UPSET. MUM NEEDS TO BE VERY CLEAR AND DIRECT BY TELLING HER EXACTLY HOW SHE IS FEELING AND WHAT SHE COULD DO TO HELP

THE GIRL WITH THE CURLY HAIR FINDS IT VERY HARD TO RECOGNISE THAT HER MUM IS UPSET THROUGH MUM'S BODY LANGUAGE AND TONE OF VOICE ALONE

TONE OF VOICE

We can use our voices in lots of ways. We can let other people know what we want and how we are feeling

We can even change our tone of voice to make someone else feel a particular way!

There are a few features of tone of voice to consider:

Feature	Description
Tone	Pitch of voice used that does not distinguish words
Inflection	Pitch of voice used that distinguishes words
Tempo	Speed of voice - how quickly or slowly someone speaks
Timbre	Quality of voice - how clear, crisp or muted
Volume	Loudness of voice - how loud, soft or quiet

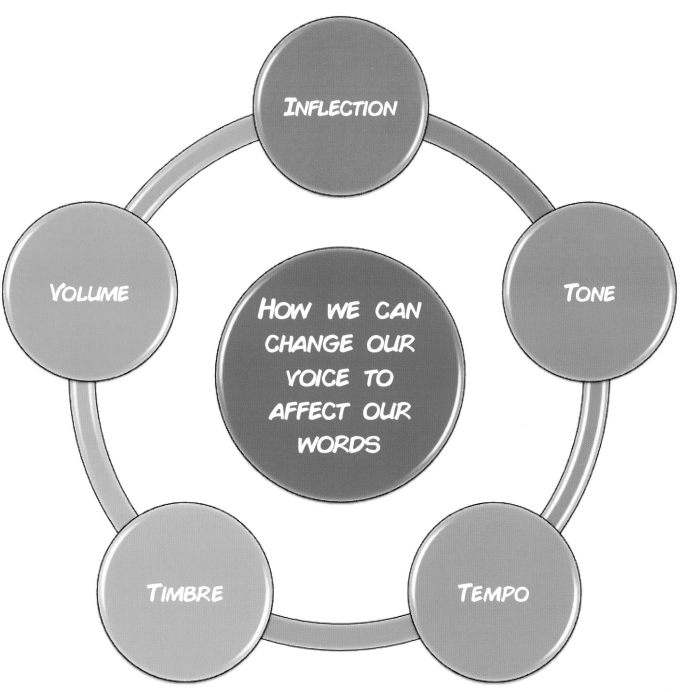

'INFLECTION' IN PARTICULAR IS
INTERESTING...

THE ENTIRE MEANING OF A SENTENCE CAN
BE CHANGED DEPENDING ON WHICH WORDS
HAVE BEEN EMPHASISED

TRY SAYING THE PHRASES ON THE
OPPOSITE PAGE, EMPHASISING THE WORDS
THAT ARE UNDERLINED. SEE IF YOU CAN
NOTICE HOW THE WHOLE MEANING OF THE
PHRASE CHANGES:

NOTICE HOW WE CAN USE WORDS IN ALL
SORTS OF WAYS

IN ASD, USING AND INTERPRETING
INFLECTION CAN BE DIFFICULT

SOMETHING TO BE AWARE OF IS THAT A
PERSON WITH ASD MAY NOT BE ABLE TO
USE IT CORRECTLY, OR MAY NOT BE ABLE
TO INTERPRET IT IN OTHERS

PERHAPS IF A PERSON WITH ASD
APPEARS UNRESPONSIVE TO WHAT SOMEONE
HAS SAID, IT MIGHT BE BECAUSE THEY
DIDN'T PICK UP ON WHAT WAS INFLECTED
IN THE VOICE

TONE OF VOICE CAN BE USED TO LET ANOTHER PERSON KNOW HOW WE ARE FEELING

OR IT CAN BE USED TO MAKE ANOTHER PERSON FEEL A PARTICULAR WAY

TRY SAYING THESE PHRASES USING DIFFERENT TONES OF VOICE AND THINK ABOUT HOW THE DIFFERENT WAYS YOU SAY THE PHRASES COULD MAKE ANOTHER PERSON FEEL:

Somebody with ASD may not pick up on the underlying emotion the other person is trying to put across

Or they might not be able to express the emotion that was intended

Consequently, a person with ASD may respond to comments or initiate conversation in an odd way

Possibly, the key is to be aware of how we might sound to others, and adapt our tone of voice so that other people respond to us in the way in which we want them to respond

25

WHEN WE KNOW SOMEONE WELL, WE CAN IDENTIFY PATTERNS, FOR EXAMPLE:

WHEN MUM IS...	THE GIRL WITH THE CURLY HAIR THINKS SHE IS...
TIRED	CROSS

WHEN THE GIRL WITH THE CURLY HAIR IS...	MUM THINKS SHE IS...
HAPPY	BORED

A GOOD COMMUNICATOR CAN LEARN TO BE AWARE OF THIS AND ADJUST THEIR COMMUNICATION ACCORDINGLY

Voice volume:

We can make words louder or quieter depending on the meaning we want to put across

We can also change the volume of our voice depending on where we are, what we are doing, and who we are speaking to

People with ASD might find it difficult to change the volume of their voice, or may not even recognise how loud or quiet their voice is

THERE ARE MANY TOOLS WE CAN USE TO LEARN HOW TO CORRECTLY USE THE VOLUME IN OUR VOICE, FOR EXAMPLE:

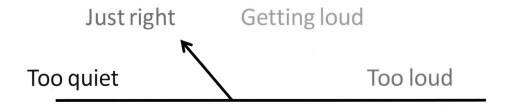

Scale	Description	Situation
0	No talking/silence	Library, bed time
1	Whispering	Telling a secret, not wanting anyone else to hear
2	Talking to someone inside	At home, in the classroom, at work
3	Talking to someone outside	In a shop, in the playground, on the street
4	Shouting	When in pain, when somebody is far away, when angry...

BODY LANGUAGE

WE CAN USE OUR BODY AND FACIAL EXPRESSIONS TO COMMUNICATE THINGS

FOR EXAMPLE, WHEN PEOPLE ARE SAD, IT'S COMMON FOR THEIR EYES TO DROOP AND FOR THEIR LIPS TO POINT DOWNWARDS

A PERSON WITH ASD MAY NOT BE ABLE TO RECOGNISE BODY LANGUAGE AND THEREFORE WILL STRUGGLE TO INTERPRET MEANINGS THAT ARE INTENDED

THEREFORE, AGAIN, WORDS ARE VERY IMPORTANT!

Common body language examples

Emotion	Body language	Facial expressions
Sadness	Slumped posture	Lack of eye contact; looking downwards; droopy eyes; downward pointing lips
Cross	Crossed arms; clenched fists	Frowning
Relaxed	Open posture	Smiling
Anxious	Fidgety; closed posture	Lack of eye contact; 'jumpy' eye contact

It might be helpful for PEOPLE WITH ASD to learn about body language so that they can try to better understand OTHERS... and so that they can be aware of the message they might be giving to others unintentionally

Body language can display quite sophisticated emotions and messages (good and bad) and can help explain the outcomes of many interactions!

NEUROTYPICAL PEOPLE COULD BE A BIT MORE OPEN TO INTERPRETING WHAT DIFFERENT BODY LANGUAGE MIGHT SIGNIFY

FOR EXAMPLE, MANY NEUROTYPICAL PEOPLE WOULD ASSUME THAT LACK OF EYE CONTACT MEANS INATTENTION AND THAT THE PERSON WITH ASD IS IGNORING THEM, HOWEVER THE PERSON WITH ASD MIGHT ACTUALLY BE PAYING CLOSE ATTENTION

WE CAN ALL WORK ON BEING MORE OPEN-MINDED AND GETTING TO KNOW EACH OTHER AS INDIVIDUALS

LOOKING FOR PATTERNS IN BODY LANGUAGE MIGHT BE A HELPFUL THING TO PRACTICE WITH PEOPLE WE KNOW AND ARE FAMILIAR WITH:

WHEN MUM IS…	SHE…
EXCITED	SMILES
ANXIOUS	FIDGETS
CROSS	CROSSES HER ARMS

WHEN THE GIRL WITH THE CURLY HAIR IS…	SHE…
EXCITED	FLAPS HER HANDS
PAYING ATTENTION	LOOKS SOMEWHERE ELSE
ANXIOUS	FIDGETS; LOOKS AWAY; LAUGHS

BOTH PEOPLE COULD LEARN TO ASK EACH OTHER HOW THEY ARE FEELING, IF THEY ARE UNSURE. IT'S OK TO ASK FOR CLARIFICATION ABOUT SOMEONE ELSE'S FEELINGS AND IT'S MUCH BETTER TO DO THIS RATHER THAN GET FRUSTRATED OR CONFUSED

Different types of communicator

IT IS THOUGHT THAT THERE ARE 4 DIFFERENT TYPES OF COMMUNICATOR (BASED ON THE VAK MODEL*):

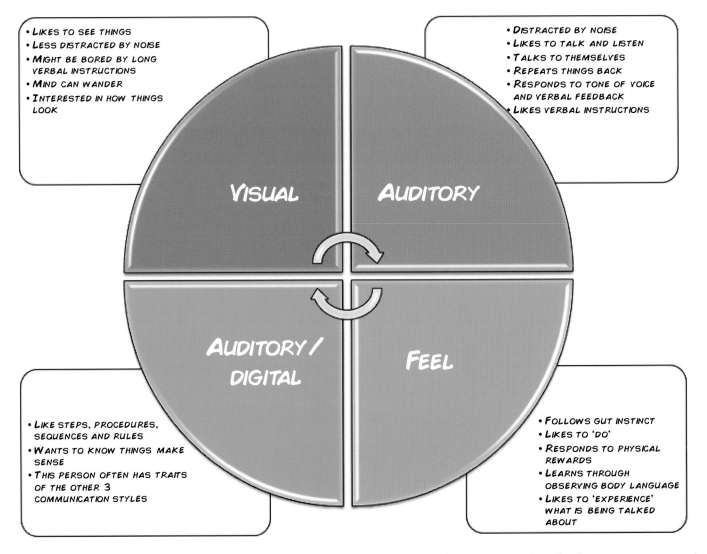

- LIKES TO SEE THINGS
- LESS DISTRACTED BY NOISE
- MIGHT BE BORED BY LONG VERBAL INSTRUCTIONS
- MIND CAN WANDER
- INTERESTED IN HOW THINGS LOOK

- DISTRACTED BY NOISE
- LIKES TO TALK AND LISTEN
- TALKS TO THEMSELVES
- REPEATS THINGS BACK
- RESPONDS TO TONE OF VOICE AND VERBAL FEEDBACK
- LIKES VERBAL INSTRUCTIONS

VISUAL

AUDITORY

AUDITORY / DIGITAL

FEEL

- LIKE STEPS, PROCEDURES, SEQUENCES AND RULES
- WANTS TO KNOW THINGS MAKE SENSE
- THIS PERSON OFTEN HAS TRAITS OF THE OTHER 3 COMMUNICATION STYLES

- FOLLOWS GUT INSTINCT
- LIKES TO 'DO'
- RESPONDS TO PHYSICAL REWARDS
- LEARNS THROUGH OBSERVING BODY LANGUAGE
- LIKES TO 'EXPERIENCE' WHAT IS BEING TALKED ABOUT

*The VAK Learning Styles Model was developed by psychologists in the 1920s to classify the most common ways that people learn

IT CAN BE HELPFUL TO WORK OUT 1) WHICH TYPE OF COMMUNICATOR WE ARE... AND 2) WHICH TYPE OF COMMUNICATOR THE PERSON IS THAT WE ARE COMMUNICATING TO

ADAPTING OUR COMMUNICATION TO MATCH HOW SOMEBODY ELSE TENDS TO COMMUNICATE IS A REALLY HELPFUL TECHNIQUE TO LEARN!

ALSO, IT'S QUITE INTERESTING TO NOTICE THAT PEOPLE ARE MORE DRAWN TO PEOPLE WHO COMMUNICATE IN A SIMILAR WAY TO THEMSELVES

(IN REALITY, MOST PEOPLE ARE PROBABLY A MIXTURE OF ALL 4 TYPES, BUT MANY PEOPLE STILL HAVE A PREFERENCE OR TENDENCY)

HOW CAN WE WORK OUT WHICH TYPE OF COMMUNICATOR WE ARE OR WHICH TYPE OTHERS ARE?

THINK ABOUT HOW YOU DESCRIBE THINGS AND LISTEN OR OBSERVE TO HOW OTHERS DESCRIBE THINGS

HERE ARE SOME EXAMPLES...

Visual communicator:

Auditory communicator:

Feel communicator:

AUDITORY / DIGITAL COMMUNICATOR:

LISTENING

LISTENING IS NOT THE SAME AS HEARING

LISTENING IS RECOGNISING AND UNDERSTANDING BOTH VERBAL AND NON-VERBAL LANGUAGE:

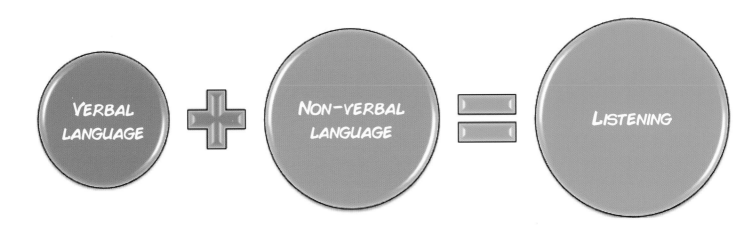

AS DESCRIBED AT THE BEGINNING OF THIS BOOK, PEOPLE WITH ASD MAY STRUGGLE WITH NON-VERBAL LANGUAGE, MAKING IT DIFFICULT FOR THEM TO LISTEN TO PEOPLE

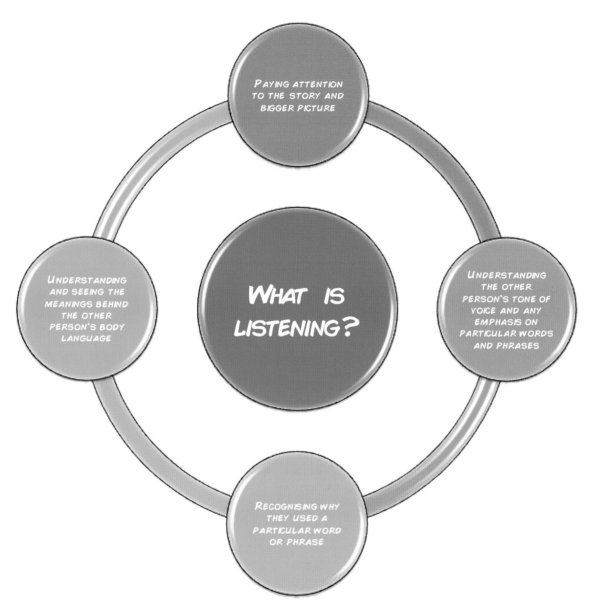

WHAT IS LISTENING?

- Paying attention to the story and bigger picture
- Understanding the other person's tone of voice and any emphasis on particular words and phrases
- Recognising why they used a particular word or phrase
- Understanding and seeing the meanings behind the other person's body language

PEOPLE WITH ASD THEREFORE MIGHT BE MORE PRONE TO HEARING RATHER THAN LISTENING

Struggling to understand non-verbal language (tone of voice and body language) means that PEOPLE WITH ASD may:

- Struggle to understand the bigger picture
- Hear words as words, rather than meanings
- Be distracted by the environment
- Lose track of what is being said
- Struggle to keep up with pace of conversation

One of the reasons I think I appear not to have much empathy or emotion for someone is because I don't fully understand what they are telling me

TIPS TO IMPROVE LISTENING SKILLS

Paraphrasing

Paraphrase what the other person has said

Paraphrasing is repeating back what somebody has said using your own words. It can be more sophisticated:

I'm not sure where we'll go this year, so long as it's somewhere hot!

I see. So Spain could be an option as it's hot?

OR VERY SIMPLE:

Summarising

Get into the habit of summarising what you have said

For example when The Girl with the Curly Hair visits the dentist, She chit chats away during the procedure... but provides a handy summary at the end:

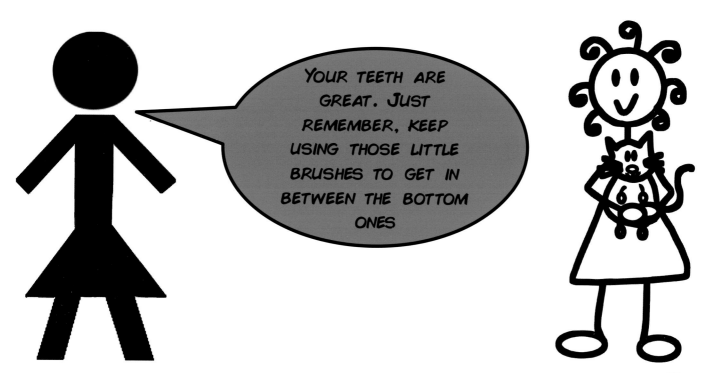

Repeating back

Repeating back is another listening technique people use. However, it may not be very effective for a person with ASD who may struggle to work out whether a statement is just a statement or whether it's prompting further conversation:

ALSO, IF A PERSON WITH ASD REPEATS WHAT HAS BEEN SAID TO THEM, BE AWARE THAT THEY MAY STRUGGLE TO USE THEIR TONE OF VOICE CORRECTLY... A PERSON WITH ASD COULD THEREFORE LEARN HOW TO USE TONE OF VOICE TO ASK QUESTIONS RATHER THAN GIVE STATEMENTS

FOR EXAMPLE, "YOU DIDN'T GET THE JOB" SOUNDS DIFFERENT AS A STATEMENT VS A QUESTION... WHEN SAID AS A QUESTION IT LEADS TO FURTHER CONVERSATION AND IS A GOOD LISTENING TECHNIQUE:

QUESTION!

WHEN SPEAKING, A GOOD COMMUNICATOR WILL ENCOURAGE AND CREATE OPPORTUNITIES FOR THE OTHER PERSON TO ASK QUESTIONS

WHEN LISTENING, A GOOD COMMUNICATOR WILL ASK QUESTIONS TO CLARIFY THINGS

LISTEN FOR MAIN IDEAS AND HIGHLIGHT THE MAIN IDEAS

ALWAYS LET THE OTHER PERSON FINISH WHAT THEY ARE SAYING (VERY IMPORTANT IN ASD/NT COMMUNICATION):

BECAUSE **I** HAVE DIFFERENT THOUGHT PROCESSES AND A DIFFERENT EXPERIENCE OF THE WORLD, IT IS EXTRA IMPORTANT FOR ME TO BE ABLE TO FINISH WHAT **I'M** SAYING

IT'S EASY FOR ANOTHER PERSON TO INTERRUPT AND ASSUME WHAT **I'M** GOING TO SAY, BASED ON WHAT THEY ARE THINKING, NOT WHAT **I** AM THINKING AND EXPERIENCING

Reduce environmental distractions

This is massively helpful for everyone!

Always consider your environment, in particular taking into consideration that someone with ASD may have hypersensitivities to smells, sounds, colours, movement, etc.

Also consider, is there enough time to fully converse?

Give full attention to the person who is speaking

Ask for factual information

A person with ASD may struggle to understand the context around what another person is saying or they may miss out on information that is implied but not explicitly said

A person with ASD can learn to ask for the facts

The other person can learn to give the facts and not assume the ASD person already has the knowledge

EMPATHY

"*Put yourselves in their shoes*"

A lot of people misunderstand what this means!

It correctly means: thinking about what something would be like for *them* to do it

As opposed to thinking about what it would be like for *you* to do it

DEVELOPING ANOTHER POINT OF VIEW WHEN WE COMMUNICATE WITH SOMEONE IS VERY IMPORTANT AND TEACHES US TO HAVE EMPATHY

THE GIRL WITH THE CURLY HAIR IS APPLYING TO A SMALL, LOCAL UNIVERSITY BECAUSE SHE DOESN'T WANT TO MOVE AWAY FROM THE AREA

BUT THE PEOPLE AROUND HER JUST CAN'T PUT THEMSELVES IN HER SHOES!

THERE ARE 3 HELPFUL WAYS WE CAN LEARN TO RELATE TO SOMEONE ELSE WHEN WE COMMUNICATE:

1) ACCEPTING THAT SOMEBODY IS A CERTAIN WAY OR HAS MADE A CERTAIN DECISION WITHOUT JUDGING THEM

2) TAKING THE TIME TO UNDERSTAND WHY THEY HAVE SAID SOMETHING OR BEHAVED IN THAT MANNER

3) RELATING BECAUSE YOU HAVE FELT THAT WAY OR BEHAVED THAT WAY YOURSELF

IT CAN BE HELPFUL TO RECOGNISE WHAT THESE LAYERS ARE AND USE THE DEEPER LAYERS WHERE WE CAN

HERE ARE EXAMPLES OF EACH OF THESE WAYS AND ALSO ONE UNHELPFUL WAY:

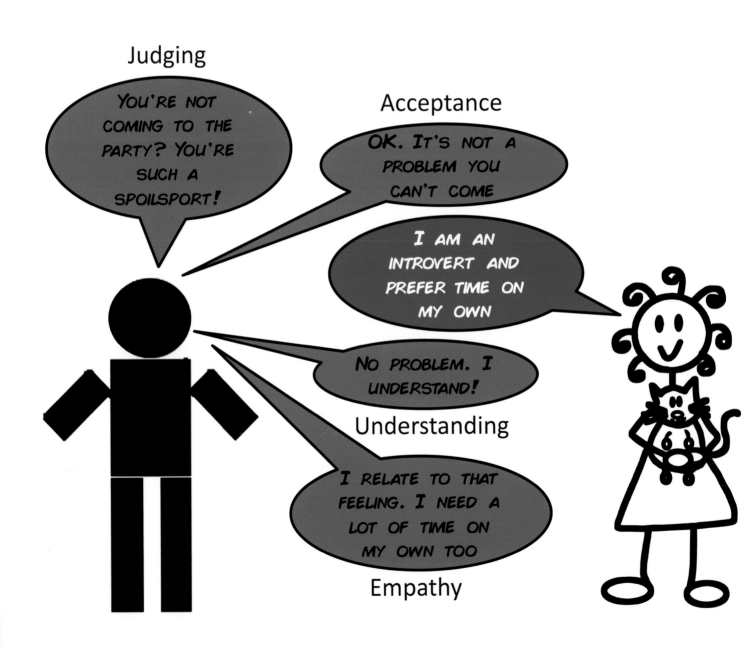

IF WE WANT TO TRULY CONNECT WITH SOMEONE, THERE IS A BIT OF RESPONSIBILITY ON OUR OWN SIDE TO GIVE SOMEONE ELSE AN EXPLANATION

A GOOD COMMUNICATOR MIGHT DEMONSTRATE ACCEPTANCE, UNDERSTANDING TOGETHER WITH EMPATHY OR SYMPATHY...

AND A GOOD COMMUNICATOR WILL ALSO BE OPEN WITH OTHERS. THE PREVIOUS EXAMPLE SHOWS THE GIRL WITH THE CURLY HAIR BEING OPEN WITH HER NEUROTYPICAL COLLEAGUE

GETTING TO THE POINT:

COMMUNICATION IS THE EXCHANGE OF INFORMATION WITHOUT THE MEANING GETTING LOST

WHEN COMMUNICATING WITH A PERSON WITH ASD, IT'S EASY FOR MEANINGS TO GET LOST!

NEUROTYPICAL PEOPLE CAN LEARN SOME GOOD TECHNIQUES GENERALLY TO REDUCE THE LIKELIHOOD OF MEANINGS GETTING LOST:

- BE DIRECT AND SAY ONE THING AT A TIME
- TRY TO STAY ON TOPIC
- REDUCE OPEN ENDED QUESTIONS
- CONSIDER, WHAT IS THE *PURPOSE* OF THIS INTERACTION? (SOMETIMES IT'S BEST NOT TO SPEAK JUST FOR THE SAKE OF SPEAKING UNLESS YOU ARE CLEAR YOU ARE DOING SO!)
- BE CONCISE
- USE ONE STATEMENT OR QUESTION AT A TIME
- ALLOW TIME AND DIRECTLY ASK FOR THE OTHER PERSON'S RESPONSE

HERE IS AN EXAMPLE OF A DIFFICULT INTERACTION FOR THE GIRL WITH THE CURLY HAIR WHEN SHE GOES INTO THE SHOP TO BUY SOMETHING. THE SHOP WORKER IS TRYING TO MAKE SMALL TALK, BUT IS DOING SO IN THE WRONG WAY, NOT EVEN ALLOWING HER A MOMENT TO RESPOND...

IT'D BE MUCH BETTER IF HE BROKE THE SENTENCES DOWN, GIVING HER TIME TO RESPOND TO EACH QUESTION DIRECTLY:

THIS IS GENERALLY A GOOD TECHNIQUE TO USE TO WHEN COMMUNICATING WITH A PERSON WITH ASD

OPEN ENDED QUESTIONS CAN SOMETIMES BE CONFUSING FOR A PERSON WITH ASD BECAUSE PUTTING THINGS INTO CONTEXT AND WORKING OUT WHAT

SOMEONE ELSE MIGHT BE THINKING CAN BE REALLY HARD. FOR EXAMPLE, COLLEAGUES WANT TO GO OUT FOR LUNCH DURING THE WORK DAY:

WELL, IT DEPENDS HOW FAR THEY WANT TO TRAVEL... WHAT TYPE OF FOOD THEY WANT TO EAT... HOW MUCH THEY WANT TO SPEND?

I WOULD JUST LIKE TO GO HOME AND BE ON MY OWN... BUT I MIGHT SEEM RUDE IF I TOLD THEM THAT

I LIKE EATING MY OWN FOOD... I FEEL VERY ANXIOUS ABOUT HAVING TO EAT OTHER THINGS

HOW ABOUT THAT NEW SANDWICH PLACE AT THE END OF THE ROAD?

A CLOSED QUESTION MIGHT HAVE BEEN BETTER:

OR EVEN A COUPLE OF CHOICES:

WHEN OTHER PEOPLE GIVE LIMITED OPTIONS, IT HELPS THE PERSON WITH ASD PUT THINGS IN CONTEXT. OPEN ENDED QUESTIONS CAN CAUSE CONFUSION:

CLOSED QUESTIONS... OR LIMITED OPTIONS MIGHT BE A BIT EASIER FOR PEOPLE ON THE AUTISTIC SPECTRUM – BE CLEAR WHAT YOU ARE OFFERING!

AND ALWAYS THINK ABOUT HOW MUCH INFORMATION IS REALLY RELEVANT AND NECESSARY FOR YOU TO GIVE TO REDUCE THE LIKELIHOOD OF CAUSING EXTRA CONFUSION:

ANOTHER TIP IS TO ALWAYS BE CLEAR ON THE *PURPOSE OF INTERACTION.* IF YOU WANT A CHAT, THAT'S FINE, BUT IF THERE IS A PARTICULAR GOAL IN MIND OR SOMETHING YOU WANT TO SAY, CLARIFY AT THE START OF THE INTERACTION:

BE DIRECT IF YOU WANT THE PERSON WITH **ASD** TO 'DO' SOMETHING. **BE** AWARE OF STATEMENTS AND OBSERVATIONS VS DIRECTIVES

REMEMBER, IF SOMEONE CAN'T PICK UP ON TONE OF VOICE, WORDS (AND QUESTIONS) ARE EXTRA IMPORTANT

IF DAD WANTS THE GIRL WITH THE CURLY HAIR TO GO AND GET SOME MILK, HE JUST NEEDS TO VERY EXPLICITLY ASK HER!

COMMUNICATION STRUCTURE

Structured communication can be helpful for everyone. Learn the steps to make a conversation more structured, for example:

- A clear start: "hello" or small talk
- Inform: telling them something
- Invite: asking them for their comments
- Listen: listening to their comments
- Acknowledge: confirming and reaffirming you've heard what they've said
- A clear end: clearly stating that you've said what you wanted to say, saying, "thanks" or saying "goodbye"

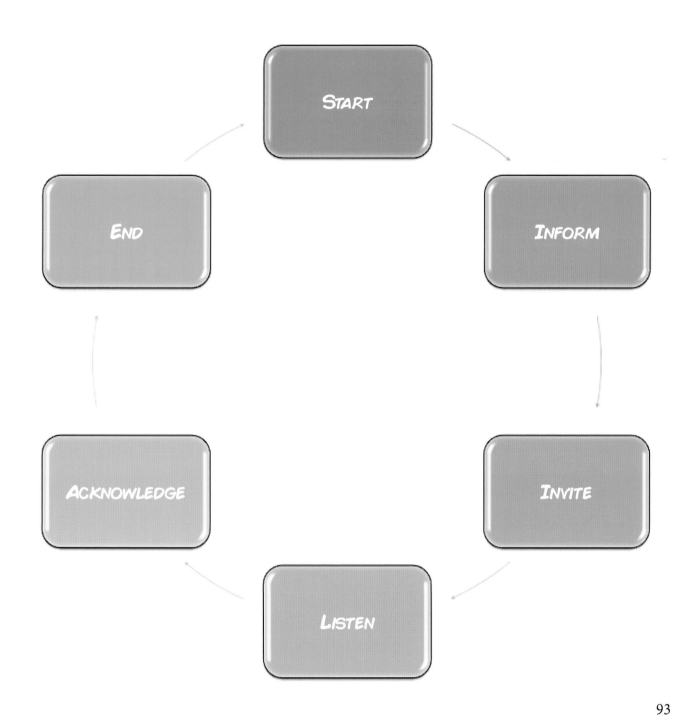

WHEN COMMUNICATING WITH SOMEBODY WITH ASD, A CLEAR INTERVAL WHERE THE PERSON CAN GIVE THEIR COMMENTS (THE INVITE SECTION) IS REALLY IMPORTANT AS OTHERWISE THEY MAY NOT KNOW HOW TO INTERJECT

SOME PEOPLE WITH ASD WILL REALLY BENEFIT FROM HAVING CLEAR STARTS AND ENDS TO A CONVERSATION

OTHERS WON'T REALLY WANT A 'START' AT ALL (AS DISCUSSED PREVIOUSLY, 'SMALL TALK' CAN OFTEN MAKE SOMEONE FEEL ANXIOUS AND GETTING TO THE POINT QUICKLY MIGHT BE A BETTER OPTION)

PROVIDING A CLEAR END CAN BE HELPFUL AS *A PERSON WITH* ASD MAY STRUGGLE TO KNOW HOW OR WHEN TO END AN INTERACTION, SO PROVIDE A CLEAR FINISH OR TRY TO BE IN TUNE WITH THEM AND END IT SO THEY DON'T HAVE TO, FOR EXAMPLE:

I'M EXHAUSTED. BUT I DON'T KNOW HOW TO END THIS MEETING

SHE LOOKS AS IF SHE'S GETTING TIRED

SHALL WE CALL IT THERE FOR TODAY?!

YES PLEASE. THANK YOU. IT WAS LOVELY TO SEE YOU

I'M SO GLAD HE SAID THAT

Some tips on starting and ending conversations, which are helpful for everyone to know:

How to start a conversation

- Say "hello"
- Some people will like small talk
- Others want you to explain very quickly what you want
- When with a person with ASD, be aware they might struggle to know how to start an interaction so be extra attentive to them
- When with a person with ASD, be very obvious that you want to talk

How to end a conversation

- Say "thanks, that's all" or "bye"
- Agree on an end time to the conversation in advance, for example agree to meet with someone for a certain amount of time or speak on the phone for a certain amount of time

The trick is really to learn the preferences of the person we are speaking with

Texting/social media:

Texting/social media might be helpful for some people with ASD as there is often no pressure for a clear start/end, it can just be a continuous exchange

Other people with ASD need obvious 'starts' ("Hello, how are you?") and 'stops' ("I've finished what I wanted to say now" or "Got to go now, bye")

Written communication:

Some good general habits when communicating with someone with ASD are to:

- Be concise
- Be specific
- Use paragraphs and line spaces
- Bullet points are useful
- Very obvious action points are useful (what and when), e.g.

> Dear The Girl with the Curly Hair,
> Please could you send out an email to all competition entrants by 13 December?
> Thank you,
> Boss

FOR NEUROTYPICAL PEOPLE, THESE HABITS ARE GOOD BECAUSE THEY MAKE YOU REALLY THINK ABOUT WHAT YOU WANT AND HELP YOU MAINTAIN GOOD FOCUS!

SUMMARY FOR NEUROTYPICAL PEOPLE

- BE AWARE OF YOUR OWN BODY LANGUAGE AND TONE OF VOICE — IF YOU ARE USING IT TO DISPLAY A CERTAIN EMOTION OR CREATE UNDERLYING MEANING, BE AWARE THE ASD PERSON MAY NOT BE ABLE TO PICK IT UP
- OPEN YOUR MIND TO DIFFERENT BODY LANGUAGE AND WHAT IT MIGHT MEAN
- SUMMARISING, PARAPHRASING AND ASKING QUESTIONS ARE GOOD TECHNIQUES TO USE WHEN COMMUNICATING
- BE AWARE OF THE ENVIRONMENT YOU ARE IN AND THINK ABOUT HOW YOU COULD REDUCE DISTRACTIONS
- BE DIRECT, BE SPECIFIC, BE CONCISE
- THINK ABOUT WHAT YOU ARE REALLY WANTING TO COMMUNICATE
- ALLOW THE PERSON ENOUGH TIME TO FINISH WHAT THEY ARE SAYING
- GIVE CLOSED OR LIMITED CHOICE QUESTIONS
- FOLLOW UP IN WRITING
- HAVE STRUCTURE IN YOUR CONVERSATION

Summary for people with ASD

- If you're unsure about anything, ask
- Summarising, paraphrasing and asking questions are good techniques to use when communicating
- Be aware of the environment you are in and think about how you could reduce distractions
- Recognise that body language and tone of voice are important and learn to use it where you can
- Have structure in your conversation

Many thanks for reading

Other books in The Visual Guides series at the time of writing:

Asperger's Syndrome
Asperger's Syndrome: Meltdowns and Shutdowns
Asperger's Syndrome in 5-8 Year Olds
Asperger's Syndrome in 8-11 Year Olds
Asperger's Syndrome in 13-16 Year Olds
Asperger's Syndrome in 16-18 Year Olds
Asperger's Syndrome for the Neurotypical Partner
Asperger's Syndrome: Social Energy
Asperger's Syndrome and Anxiety
Asperger's Syndrome: Helping Siblings
Asperger's Syndrome and Puberty
Asperger's Syndrome: Meltdowns and Shutdowns (2)
Adapting Health Therapies for People on the Autism Spectrum
Asperger's Syndrome and Emotions

New titles are continually being produced so keep an eye out!